Asset Commonality and Systemic Risk Among Large Banks in the United States

Abstract: In this paper, we present a compellingly simple yet innovative approach to capturing the buildup of systemic risk associated with commonalities in banks' asset holdings. We draw on a growing strand of theoretical literature that studies the systemic externalities of banks' balance sheet asset side allocations. By applying data aggregation and clustering techniques to publically available balance sheet data, we uncover interesting patterns in the asset holdings of the major bank holding companies in the United States during the years 2001–2013. We augment our findings with theoretical analysis and insight. Based on our analysis, we construct a novel measure of systemic risk, ACRISK, where AC stands for asset commonality. This measure captures well the buildup of systemic risk that culminated in the global credit crisis, and provides empirical support to the asset commonality theoretical notions.

1.   Introduction

Systemic risk is recognized by its aftermath: widespread failures that disrupt the proper functioning of the financial system and spill over to other sectors of the economy. The 2007-2009 global financial crisis and its devastating repercussions vividly illustrate the enormous social costs inflicted by systemic risk. These costs highlight the importance of devising measures that allow regulators and policymakers to detect and monitor systemic risk in the financial system.

Although easily recognized ex-post, systemic risk's complex and multifaceted nature makes its ex-ante detection a challenging task. The concept of systemic risk is one of the most enigmatic in economic theory, and although the literature abounds with systemic risk definitions, there is no widely-accepted definition of the term.[1] In this paper, we refer to systemic risk as the risk of significant disruptions to the proper functioning of the financial system.[2] The materialization of systemic risk requires (1) an initial shock and (2) fragility of the financial system (henceforth, system fragility). By system fragility, we refer to the predisposition of the financial system to break down if impacted by a small shock.[3] This predisposition is the product of vulnerabilities, which can include macro imbalances (e.g., excessive credit expansion), financial imbalances (e.g., asset bubbles), and distress dependencies between financial institutions, all of which create prospective "breaklines" and conduits for the transmission and propagation of shocks. Greater system fragility implies higher systemic risk, as the financial system would be less likely to withstand a potential shock. Thus, pre-spotting and monitoring system fragility should give regulators and policymakers a handle on systemic risk.

The post-crisis literature offers a profusion of quantitative approaches to capturing system fragility. These reflect the multifaceted nature of system fragility and suggest a single quantitative measure is unlikely to fully capture all the vulnerabilities in the financial system (for

---

[1] The literature offers a variety of definitions for the term "systemic risk." See Bisias et al. (2012) and De Bandt and Hartman (2000) for a survey of systemic risk definitions, origins, and mechanisms.

[3] According to Allen and Gale (2004), financial fragility is the extent to which "small shocks have disproportionately large effects." Lagunoff and Schreft (2001) refer to financial fragility as "the financial system's susceptibility to large-scale financial crises caused by small, routine economic shocks."

further discussion, see Bisais et al. [2012]). As our theoretical understanding of system fragility continues to evolve, this process should be mirrored by the construction of new empirical measures. A growing strand of recent theoretical literature, featuring papers such as Wagner (2008, 2009, and 2010), Beale et al. (2011), and Ibragimov et al. (2011), has been focusing on commonalities in banks' asset holdings as a source of system fragility.

In this paper, we focus on the system fragility that stems from asset commonality, i.e., the overlap in firms' asset portfolios. This overlap is indicative of potential distress dependencies between firms, which contribute to system fragility, and thereby to systemic risk. The major types of distress dependencies are common exposures, interconnections, and perceived distress dependencies. Common exposures exist when the assets that banks hold expose them to the same underlying risks. These, in turn, increase the likelihood and impact of simultaneous joint failures. Asset commonality straightforwardly implies the existence of common exposures among firms. Interconnections between financial firms include bilateral and multilateral relations, contracts, and transactions, all of which allow the firms to diversify and share risks, and thereby to dissipate and absorb moderate shocks. Under strenuous conditions, however, these very same interconnections can become conduits of contagion, i.e., self-amplifying transmission of distress and losses across the financial system (De Vries [2005]). Asset commonality can, at least in part, be the product of interconnections, and thus indicate the risk of contagion. Perceived distress dependencies between firms arise when partially informed market participants believe the firms to be interconnected or exposed to the same underlying risks. Such belief can lead to informational spillovers and become self-fulfilling if market participants deem the distress of one firm signifies the financial health of the other may be compromised. Perceived distress dependencies are typically spurred by similarities and commonalities among firms.[4] Asset commonality can therefore be suggestive of the risk of informational spillover.

The purpose of this paper is to propose a methodology for measuring asset commonality driven system fragility. To that end, we focus on publicly available balance sheet data of U.S. bank

---

[4] A good example for informational spillover due to perceived distress dependencies is the failures of Bear Stearns and Lehman Brothers in 2008. Although the two investment giants were hardly interconnected, their similar traits led market participants to believe that the distress of one was indicative of the other's financial health.

holding companies (BHC) with total assets of $50 billion and above in the years 2001–2013. Our sample consists of 55 firms. To ensure ample data granularity, we identify 17 asset classes. The methodology we offer is designed for multidimensional datasets. Because by their nature, such datasets could potentially be subject to data scarcity problems, we apply data aggregation techniques. We represent the information in the original dataset by aggregating it into two dimensions. The first dimension captures the concentration within the portfolio, and hence, to a certain extent, the idiosyncratic risk thereof. The second dimension indicates the extent by which the portfolio overlaps with the sample-wide aggregate portfolio, therefore representing the portfolio's risk of failing jointly with the aggregate portfolio. Our data aggregation technique works properly, as is evident from the separation of the firms into three distinct groups, which we term money center banks, lending firms, and nontraditional firms. For instance, the money center banks, which consist of the largest and most diversified firms, appear to be the most closely aligned and therefore more likely to fail jointly with the aggregate portfolio. The nontraditional firms (such as investment banks and brokers-dealers), albeit highly diversified, are nevertheless positioned further away from the aggregate portfolio, and are therefore less likely to fail jointly with it. We present a theoretical analysis that provides insight into our observations.

We implement cluster analysis techniques to capture the degree of cross-firm portfolio homogeneity. Greater homogeneity indicates that the firms' portfolios are more overlapped, which in turn suggests greater asset commonality driven system fragility. Based on this analysis, we construct a novel measure, ACRISK, which traces the evolution of system fragility associated with commonalities in banks' asset holdings. This measure is unique in that it is based solely on publicly available balance sheet information. ACRISK, which is a low frequency measure, performs well in comparison with a well-known high frequency measure, the SRISK index, by Engle and Brownlees (2011). ACRISK could be instrumental in allowing regulators and policymakers to monitor and contain systemic risk.

This paper is organized as follows. Section 2 reviews the relevant literature. Section 3 provides a description of the data and discusses the challenges associated with high dimensionality datasets. Section 4 presents the measures of concentration and dispersion we use. Section 5 describes our observations. Section 6 presents the analytical relationship between portfolio concentration and dispersion. Section 7 explains our observations using the analytical relationships presented in section 6. Section 8 describes the cluster analysis of our data and constructs our measure of asset commonality driven systemic risk, ACRISK. Section 9 evaluates the performance of ACRISK. Section 10 concludes.

2. Related Literature

Our paper is related to two strands of the literature: empirical systemic risk literature and asset commonality literature. The 2007–2009 financial crisis sparked a flurry of research activity which resulted in a vast variety of quantitative approaches to measuring systemic risk. Rodriguez-Moreno and Pena (2013) divide these measures into two categories: high frequency measures, which are derived from market data, and low frequency measures, which are based on balance sheet data or macroeconomic aggregates. High frequency measures are designed for real-time monitoring of market variables and sentiments, which should ideally allow the identification of the point in time in which systemic risk materializes, either at the firm or the system level. The literature offers a wide variety of high frequency measures. Huang et al. (2009) use credit default swaps spreads and equity prices to measure the probabilities of default and asset return correlations of financial firms. Adrian and Brunnermeier (2011) use market data to construct the CoVaR measure, which is the financial system's value at risk conditional on an individual institution being in distress. Acharya et al. (2010b) introduce the systemic expected shortfall index, which measures the decline in a firm's stock price conditional on a large one-day drop in market prices, and the Marginal Expected Shortfall (MES), which captures a firm's losses in the tail of the system's loss distribution. Engle and Brownlees (2011) construct the SRISK index by supplementing the MES with firm leverage and size information.

Low frequency measures, according to Rodriguez-Moreno and Pena (2013), are geared toward tracking the evolution of potential imbalances in the economy or within individual firms. If successful, low frequency measures should capture the buildup of fragility in the financial system and serve as leading indicators. The literature offers a range of low frequency measures. The International Monetary Fund uses "Financial Soundness Indicators," which are calculated as various balance sheet ratios, to capture the soundness of the financial system in different countries (see San Jose et al. [2008]). Borio and Lowe (2002) and Borio and Drehmann (2009) develop a series of gap indicators based on the simultaneous deviations of key variables, such as credit to gross domestic product (GDP), real asset prices, and private sector leverage, from their historical trend. Schwaab et al. (2011) propose a set of coincident measures that are based on macro financial and credit risk data and use misalignments between credit risk conditions and macroeconomic fundamentals as early warning indicators for financial distress. The measure we propose is based exclusively on balance sheet information. Because of this, our measure belongs to the low frequency category of systemic risk measures. We take a cluster analysis approach to capturing the overlaps in firms' asset portfolios and use the results of our analysis to construct a measure of asset commonality driven systemic risk.

Our paper is also closely related to the asset commonality literature, which studies the systemic implications of commonalities in financial firms' asset holdings. This growing body of theoretical literature is based on the notion that overlaps in financial firms' asset portfolios increase distress dependencies between them, and thereby the likelihood of multiple failures. Given that the number of available asset classes is finite, portfolio diversification on the part of individual firms increases the prevalence of overlaps, and thereby of systemic risk (Wagner [2008 and 2010], Beale et al. [2011]). Since conventional wisdom has it that diversification decreases firm-specific risk of default, there might exist a tradeoff between idiosyncratic risk and systemic risk. Empirical evidence supports this idea: according to De Jonghe (2009), diversified financial institutions have higher tail dependence. The relationship between diversification and portfolio overlaps also suggests that the portfolio composition choices of individual firms project systemic externalities. Firms engage in societally excessive diversification either because they are oblivious of these externalities (as in Wagner [2008, 2009, and 2010], Beale et al. [2011], and Ibragimov et al. [2011]), or because they are faced with an incentive structure which, together with their limited liability, propels them to correlate with their peers (as in Acharya and Yorulmazer [2005 and 2007]).

Our paper brings to the data the notions of the asset commonality literature and offers an empirical methodology for capturing asset commonality driven system fragility based on those notions. We aggregate the data into two dimensions that differentiate portfolio diversification from portfolio overlaps. Our observations provide a confirmation for the notion of tradeoff between idiosyncratic risk and systemic risk. The firms in our sample that are more highly diversified tend to overlap more with the aggregate portfolio, indicating that they are more prone to failing jointly with the market. We construct a measure based on the notion that the extent to which firms' portfolios overlap is indicative of systemic risk. The fact that our measure performs well provides an empirical confirmation of this notion.

3.   Data

Our ideal dataset would have covered both BHCs and financial holding companies (FHC), and spanned both balance sheet and off-balance sheet asset holdings. Off-balance sheet data for both BHCs and FHCs is unavailable, however, and the limited granularity of historical balance sheet data for FHCs excludes them from our sample. We therefore limit ourselves to BHC balance sheet data. We focus on large, complex U.S. BHCs with total consolidated assets of $50 billion and above from the first quarter of 2001 to the first quarter of 2013. In doing so we follow the Dodd–Frank Wall Street Reform and Consumer Protection Act, which sets a $50 billion threshold for systemically important financial institution designation. Our sample comprises 55 firms, some of which enter or leave the sample at some point during the sample period. We obtained balance sheet data from the Quarterly Unified BHC Performance Reports (PRISM), and focus on 17 balance sheet items (henceforth referred to as asset classes). Despite their obvious relevance to the buildup of financial fragility, off-balance sheet assets are not included due to lack of data. For each quarter, we aggregate the portfolios of all the firms in our sample to obtain an aggregate portfolio. We consider the aggregate portfolio to be a representation of the market, broadly defined.

Since our analysis focuses on portfolio composition commonalities, we calculate for each bank in each quarter the weights assigned to the different asset classes within the portfolio. We thereby obtain vectors of weights that are used as inputs in our subsequent analysis. The aggregate portfolio is also given in weights. Since by definition the weights of asset classes within a portfolio sum up to one, there is dependence between the weights. This implies that the number of degrees of freedom in our dataset is 16. In other words, the original dataset is a 16-dimensional simplex within the 17-dimensional space.

A well-known challenge often prevalent in high dimensional datasets is the curse of dimensionality (Donoho [2000]). To be more specific, traditional statistical tools tend to perform poorly when applied to high dimensional datasets. As dimensionality increases, the volume of the space containing the data sample increases much faster than the available data so that the data quickly become sparse. To obtain statistically sound and reliable results, the amount of data needed should grow exponentially with dimensionality. The curse of dimensionality problem can be addressed by means of dimensionality reduction techniques, such as dimension removal or aggregation. For a comprehensive survey of dimension reduction techniques, we refer the reader to Fodor (2002). The use of more granular balance sheet data, resulting in a larger number of asset classes, could give rise to a more severe manifestation of the problem.

One way of addressing the above challenges is to aggregate the information embedded in the 17-dimensional dataset. Although this could be achieved by various techniques, we opted to summarize the information using two measures: the well-known Herfindahl Hirschman Index (HHI) and the Dispersion Index (DI). Section 4 provides the formulaic definitions of these indices and elaborates on their role in our analysis.

4.   Measures of Concentration and Dispersion

We use the HHI to measure the concentration of each firm's asset portfolio. The HHI of firm i is the sum of the squares of the weights of the asset classes within the firm's portfolio:

$$HHI_{i,t} = \sum_{k=1}^{m} W_{i,k,t}^2, \qquad i = 1, \dots, n_t, \tag{1}$$

where $W_{i,k,t}$ is the weight of asset class k in firm i's portfolio in time t, m is the number of asset classes, and n_t is the number of firms in time t.

We adopt the conventional wisdom according to which higher portfolio concentration implies a higher idiosyncratic risk of failure. We therefore use the HHI of a firm in a given quarter as an indicator of its idiosyncratic risk of failure. The HHI resonates with the micro-prudential supervision of banks, which emphasizes the importance of well diversified asset portfolios to the safety and soundness of individual firms.

The 2007–2009 global crisis highlighted the need to supplement the existing micro-prudential regulatory framework with a macro-prudential one. In the United States, the Dodd–Frank Act mandates the Federal supervisors employ both the micro- and macro-prudential supervision and regulation of financial institutions. This newly assigned role of safeguarding the stability of the financial system needs to be informed by horizontal, cross-firm measures and indicators. Our second measure, the DI, serves this purpose. We define DI as the square of the Euclidean distance between a firm's portfolio and the aggregate portfolio, where the aggregate portfolio is an artificial reference point defined as the sample-wide aggregate portfolio in each quarter

$$DI_{i,t} = \sum_{k=1}^{m}\left(W_{i,k,t} - W_{k,t}\right)^2, \tag{2}$$

where $W_{k,t}$ is the weight of asset class k in the aggregate portfolio in time t.

Technically, the DI measures the distance between the diversification pattern of an individual firm's portfolio and that of the aggregate portfolio. The lower the value of a firm's *DI*, the closer its diversification pattern is to that of the aggregate portfolio. In other words, the lower a firm's *DI*, the greater its asset commonality with the aggregate portfolio, which in turn implies that the firm would stand a higher risk of failing with the market should the latter be hit by a systemic shock. The DI of a firm is therefore inversely related to its 'systemicness.' The DI not only indicates where each firm's portfolio stands vis à vis the aggregate portfolio, but also allows firm-to-firm comparisons. The information provided by the DI is therefore invaluable to macro-prudential surveillance.

The informational content of our dataset is folded into two dimensions: an idiosyncratic, portfolio-specific dimension, captured by the HHI, and a systemic dimension, captured by the DI. Ciciretti and Corvino (2011) use the above two indices in a regression analysis study of systemic risk among balanced investment funds. Our approach is different. We use the HHI and DI to aggregate firms' asset portfolio data with the aims of identifying diversification patterns among the firms and constructing a measure that captures asset commonality driven systemic risk. In the next section, we explore the patterns and dynamics exhibited by the firms in our sample in the two dimensional (DI, HHI) plane.

5. Observed Diversification Patterns

We study the firms' portfolio diversification patterns in the two dimensional (DI, HHI) plane. We find that the firms display a persistent configuration in the (DI, HHI) plane over the entire sample period:

- The firms form a leaning U-shape configuration with the base of the U pointing at the origin. Along the U-shape configuration, we observe three distinct groups: one populating the base, and the other two each populating an arm (see figure 1).
- The firms positioned along the upper arm display high HHI and moderate DI values, whereas those positioned along the lower arm are typically characterized by low HHI and high DI values. The firms along the base, which are the closest to the aggregate portfolio, demonstrate low HHI and DI values.
- The upper arm has a clear and persistent positive slope over the sample period.

Figure 1. The Industry Configuration in the (DI, HHI) Plane, 2009Q1, with Firms by Tickers and the Aggregate Portfolio Denoted by *A*.

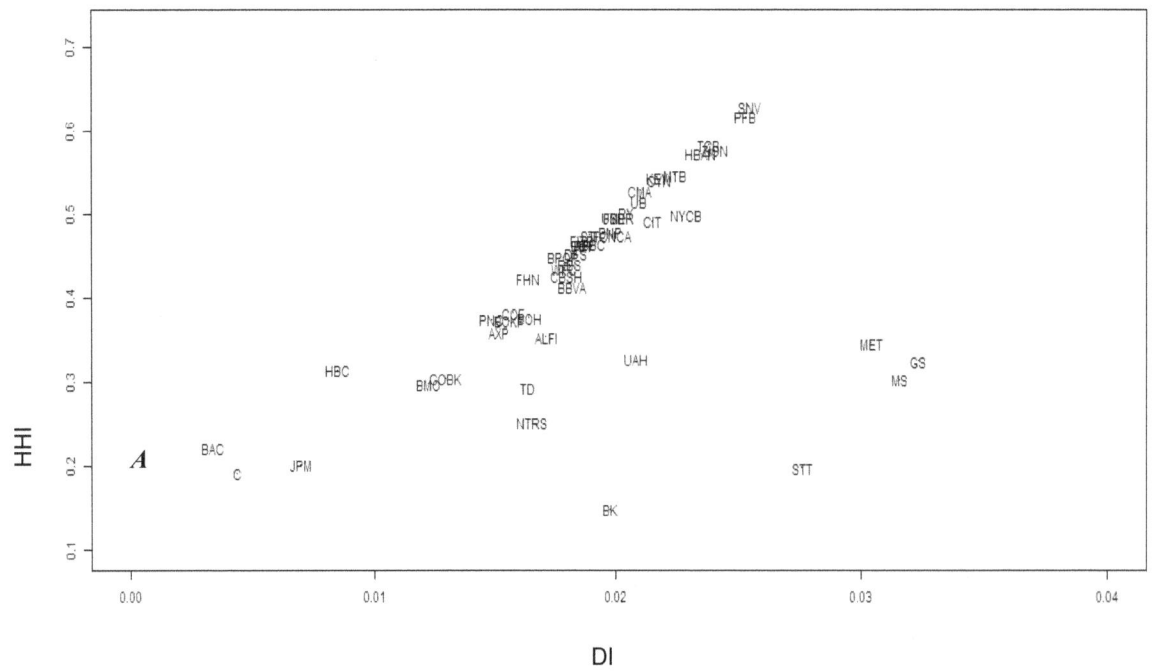

Business model categories are central to our analysis. We identify three business model categories which demonstrate distinct portfolio (DI, HHI) patterns: lending firms, money center banks, and non-traditional firms. The lending firm business model category comprises depository institutions, savings and loans firms, mortgage lenders, and credit card companies, all of which rely heavily on the traditional banking activities of borrowing from and lending to households and the private sector. The business models associated with lending firms imply certain limitations on the composition of their asset portfolios, and constrain the extent to which they can diversify. Therefore, their portfolios are significantly more concentrated than the aggregate portfolio. We find the upper arm to be populated almost exclusively by lending firms.

The money center bank business model category comprises banking giants that are typically heavily engaged in borrowing and lending to governments, financial institutions, and large corporations, and are prominent players in both national and international financial markets. Their business models span a broad range of traditional and non-traditional banking activities, resulting in highly diversified asset portfolios. This business model category includes some of the largest firms in our sample, such as Citi, Bank of America, and J.P. Morgan. Due to their sizable balance sheets, these firms constitute a substantial portion of—and hereby define—the aggregate portfolio. The close similarity between money center banks' portfolios and the aggregate portfolio is indicated by their proximity to the aggregate portfolio in the (DI, HHI) plane. We find the group closest to the aggregate portfolio to be populated almost exclusively by money center banks.

The non-traditional firm business model category is a catchall for all nontraditional business models in our sample. This business model category comprises a heterogeneous mix of business models, namely processing banks, investment brokers, asset managers, foreign banks, and one life insurer. Despite the substantial differences in their individual business models, these firms nevertheless demonstrate a common tendency to be more diversified than the lending firms, and to position themselves away from the aggregate portfolio. We find the lower arm to be populated predominantly by non-traditional firms.

Finally, the lending firms constituting the upper arm appear to be aligned to the right of an imaginary straight line with a persistent, positive slope (see figure 1). This alignment could indicate the existence of an implicit frontier limiting these firms' diversification choices as reflected in the (DI, HHI) plane. This frontier needs to be identified and explained. The lower arm, populated by the non-traditional firms, also has a positive, albeit less persistent, slope. This alignment could suggest the existence of yet another implicit frontier. Another important observation is the wide, unpopulated area between the two arms. In section 6, we offer a theoretical framework for explaining the above observations. Our theoretical framework focuses on the mathematical relation between DI and HHI and the diversification constraints projected by the firms' business models.

6.   The Mathematical Relation Between Concentration and Dispersion

The following mathematical relation between DI and HHI is critical in understanding the diversification patterns of lending firms, money center banks, and non-traditional firms:

$$DI_{i,t} = HHI_{i,t} + HHI_t - 2 \sum_{k=1}^{m} W_{i,k,t} \, W_{k,t} \,, \tag{3}$$

where HHI_t denotes the HHI of the aggregate portfolio in time t.

To analyze the implications of the above formula to patterns of diversification, we introduce the notations $\boldsymbol{W}_{i,t} = (W_{i,1,t}, \ldots, W_{i,m,t})$ and $\boldsymbol{W}_t = (W_{1,t}, \ldots, W_{m,t})$ representing the vectors of weights of firm i's portfolio and the aggregate portfolio, respectively. For any vectors of weights $\boldsymbol{W}_{i,t}$ and $\boldsymbol{W}_t$, the following inequalities hold:

$$\boldsymbol{W}_{i,t} \cdot \boldsymbol{W}_t = \sum_{k=1}^{m} W_{i,k,t} \, W_{k,t} \geq 0 \tag{4}$$

$$\boldsymbol{W}_{i,t} \cdot \boldsymbol{W}_t \leq \sqrt{HHI_{i,t}} \cdot \sqrt{HHI_t} \tag{5}$$

Inequality (4) is the direct result of the weights being nonnegative, while (5) is the Cauchy-Schwarz inequality. Note that for $\sum_{k=1}^{m} W_{i,k,t} \, W_{k,t} = 0$ to hold, that is, for $\boldsymbol{W}_{i,t}$ to be orthogonal to $\boldsymbol{W}_t$, either $W_{i,k,t}$ or $W_{k,t}$ should be zero for every asset class k. Given that in practice, however, the aggregate portfolio is highly diversified and therefore assigns a strictly positive weight to every asset class, $\sum_{k=1}^{m} W_{i,k,t} \, W_{k,t}$ is strictly positive.

We now proceed to a formulaic description of the lower and upper frontiers for the DI and HHI configurations, the existence of which was implied by our observations in the previous section.

6.1 The Lower Frontier

The following proposition identifies the lower frontier in the (DI, HHI) plane.

Proposition 1. *An immediate implication of (3) and (4) is that*

$$DI_{i,t} \leq HHI_{i,t} + HHI_{M,t}. \tag{6}$$

The equality

$$DI_{i,t} = HHI_{i,t} + HHI_{M,t} \tag{7}$$

holds only when the vectors $\boldsymbol{W}_{i,t}$ and $\boldsymbol{W}_t$ are orthogonal.

We henceforth refer to line (7) as the lower frontier. Inequality (6) shows that for any given level of $DI_{i,t}$, $HHI_{i,t}$ should lie on line (6) or above it. Given that in practice, however, $\sum_{k=1}^{m} W_{i,k,t} W_{k,t}$ is strictly positive, a firm cannot construct a portfolio that is orthogonal to the aggregate portfolio. This implies that firms can position themselves close to the lower frontier, but not on it.

6.2 The Upper Frontier

The following proposition identifies the frontier in the (DI, HHI) plane that constrains the set of firms populating the upper arm.

Proposition 2. *For the vectors $\boldsymbol{W}_{i,t}$ and $\boldsymbol{W}_t$, the following inequality always holds:*

$$\sqrt{DI_{i,t}} \geq \sqrt{HHI_{i,t}} - \sqrt{HHI_t}. \tag{8}$$

The equality

$$\sqrt{DI_{i,t}} = \sqrt{HHI_{i,t}} - \sqrt{HHI_t} \tag{9}$$

is achieved only when $\boldsymbol{W}_{i,t} = \boldsymbol{W}_t$. Note that this suggests that equality (9) is obtained only at one point in the (*DI, HHI*) plane: the point at which $DI_{i,t} = 0$ and $HHI_{i,t} = HHI_t$.
Proof. From (3) and (5) we obtain the following inequality

$$DI_{i,t} \geq HHI_{i,t} + HHI_t - 2\sqrt{HHI_{i,t}} \cdot \sqrt{HHI_t} \tag{10}$$

We refer to line (9) as the upper frontier.

Figure 2 depicts the configuration of the firms in our sample in the first quarter of 2009.

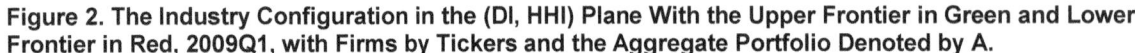

Figure 2. The Industry Configuration in the (DI, HHI) Plane With the Upper Frontier in Green and Lower Frontier in Red, 2009Q1, with Firms by Tickers and the Aggregate Portfolio Denoted by A.

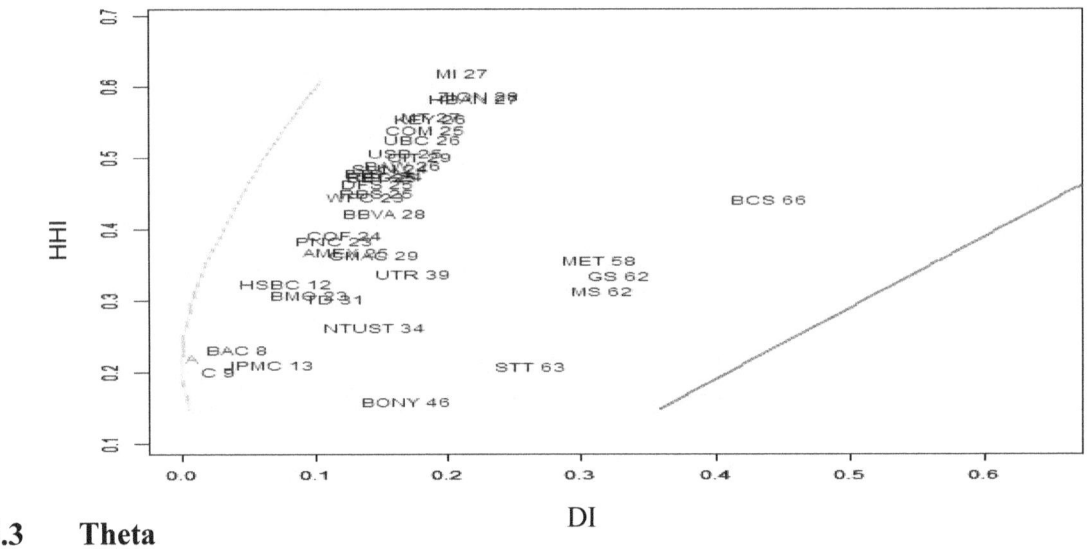

6.3 Theta

In this subsection, we introduce an additional measure for capturing the divergence of a firm's portfolio from the aggregate portfolio. We refer to this measure as $\theta_{i,t}$, the angular distance between a firm i's portfolio and the aggregate portfolio at time t. To derive this measure, we start with the following well-known property of dot products

$$\boldsymbol{W}_{i,t} \cdot \boldsymbol{W}_t = \sqrt{HHI_{i,t}} \cdot \sqrt{HHI_t} \cdot \cos(\theta_{i,t}) \tag{11}$$

where $\theta_{i,t}$ is the angle between the vectors $\boldsymbol{W}_{i,t}$ and $\boldsymbol{W}_t$. Plugging the last identity into (3) we obtain

$$DI_{i,t} = HHI_{i,t} + HHI_t - 2\sqrt{HHI_{i,t}} \cdot \sqrt{HHI_t} \cdot \cos(\theta_{i,t}) \tag{12}$$

Theta ranges between 0 (the firm's portfolio weights are identical to those of the aggregate portfolio) and 90 (the firm's vector of portfolio weights is orthogonal to that of the aggregate portfolio). The importance of theta to our analysis stems from the fact that the upper and lower frontiers identified above are defined by the two extreme values of theta. Specifically, the upper frontier is defined by $\theta = 0$ degree, whereas the lower frontier, which requires that

$\sum_{k=1}^{m} W_{i,k,t} \, W_{k,t} = 0$, can be achieved only when $\theta = 90$ degrees.

Figure 2 shows that the lending firms are relatively close to the upper frontier, whereas the non-traditional firms are closer to the lower frontier. Calculated θ values clearly indicate that the diversification patterns of the lending firms are closer to the aggregate portfolio than those of the non-traditional firms. This is not as obvious from the firms' positions in the (*DI, HHI*) plane alone.

The θ measure adds an additional layer of information and complements our observations in the (DI, HHI) plane. It is, however, important to emphasize that while θ measures the angle between a firm's portfolio and the aggregate portfolio, it does not capture the position of the firm's portfolio in the (DI, HHI) plane. Two portfolios that share the same θ value may have substantially different DI and HHI values. This is clearly illustrated in figure 3, which depicts iso θ lines in the (DI, HHI) plane in the first quarter of 2009.

Because the θ measure does not provide information about the position of a portfolio in the (DI, HHI) plane, we cannot use the average θ value over all firms in the sample as a measure of asset commonality driven systemic risk. Average θ values are nevertheless useful once firms' positions in the (DI, HHI) plane have been accounted for, such as by calculating average θ values for each group of firms separately. The average θ varies substantially between the different groups: 7.4 degrees to 18.2 degrees for money center banks, 13.7 degrees to 28 degrees for lending firms, and 55 degrees to 64.9 degrees for non-traditional firms. In other words, the average θ measure shows that the money center banks are the closest to the aggregate portfolio. The lending firms are closer to the aggregate portfolio than the non-traditional firms, yet not as close as the money center banks. These findings resonate with Billio et al. (2010), who suggest that banks contribute more to fragility in the financial system than non-banks.

Figure 3. The Industry Configuration in the (DI, HHI) Plane Against Select Iso Theta Lines, 2009Q1, With Firms by Tickers and the Aggregate Portfolio Denoted by *A*.

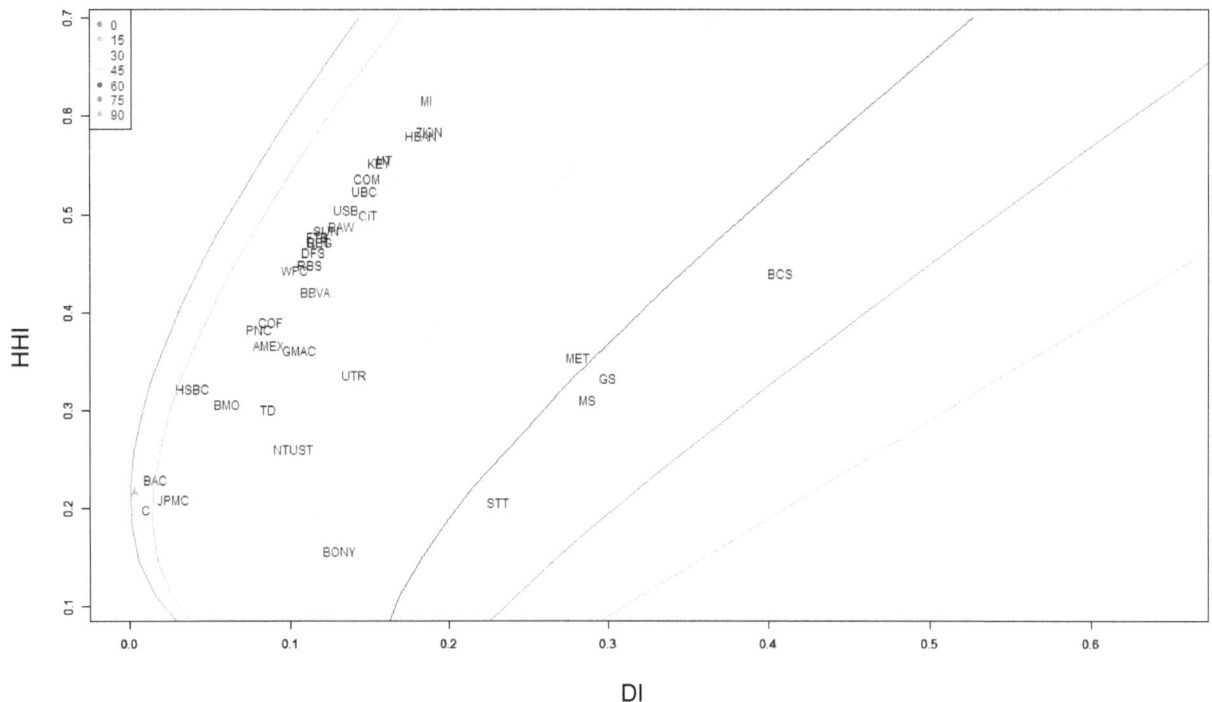

7.   Deciphering Our Observations

The mathematical relations between DI and HHI established in section 6 and summarized in propositions 1 and 2 shed light on the observed diversification patterns of the firms in our sample.

7.1   Money Center Banks

The firms closest to the aggregate portfolio comprise those we classify as money center banks. The proximity of the money center banks to the aggregate portfolio is reflected by their HHI levels, which are very close to the aggregate portfolio's, as well as their low DI and θ values.

Money center banks' proximity to the aggregate portfolio is partly explained by their size, due to which these firms dominate and define the aggregate portfolio. Yet if size alone was the reason the largest firms in our sample are also the closest to the aggregate portfolio, we would expect to find Wells Fargo, which is among the largest firms in our sample, to be close to the aggregate portfolio. Nevertheless, Wells Fargo turns out to have a portfolio that substantially diverges from the aggregate portfolio, and which places it among the lending firms. Therefore, size alone is not the explanation for the money center banks' proximity to the aggregate portfolio. The considerable flexibility of money center banks' business models implies that their proximity to the aggregate portfolio is the result of a strategy geared toward comoving closely with the market. Why would a money center bank wish to rise and fall with the market? We believe that the answer to this question lies in a reasoning close in spirit to Acharya and Yorulmazer (2005). Given their large size, money center banks are likely to have a "too big to fail" self-perception. If indeed they expect to be bailed out when it is absolutely necessary, the downside of their strategy—a high risk of joint failure—appears to be outweighed by its advantages, namely the ability to better exploit market upswings and compete with peers.

7.2   Non-Traditional Firms

The lower arm, which consists almost exclusively of firms we classify as non-traditional, is aligned with relative proximity to the lower frontier. Proposition 1 shows that the lower frontier, defined by equality (7), is achieved when a firm builds a portfolio that is orthogonal to the aggregate portfolio. The non-traditional firms' alignment close to the lower frontier is reflected in their θ values, which range between 55 degrees and 64.9 degrees, and are the highest among the firms in our sample. The non-traditional firms in our sample are highly diversified, as reflected in their low HHI levels. Nevertheless, we find these firms' diversification patterns to be significantly different from the diversification pattern displayed by the aggregate portfolio. Since the non-traditional firms' business model should allow them ample flexibility in constructing their asset portfolios, our observations could suggest that their strategies are designed to differentiate them from the aggregate portfolio. Proposition 1 shows that full orthogonality with respect to the aggregate portfolio is achieved when the scalar (or, dot) product

$W_{i,t} \cdot W_t = \sum_{k=1}^{17} W_{i,k,t} W_{k,t}$ equals zero. The aggregate portfolio is a highly diversified portfolio that assigns a positive weight to all asset classes. Thus, a firm's portfolio can never be fully orthogonal to the aggregate portfolio. In view of this, inequality (6) suggests that firms should be positioned above the frontier given by equality (7). The alignment of the non-traditional firms close to the lower frontier could suggest that their asset diversification strategies are geared toward dissociating themselves from the aggregate portfolio. It may be that despite their size, these firms do not perceive themselves as likely recipients of government aid in the event of a market crisis. The non-traditional firms may also lack the incentive to survive jointly with the market if the profitability of their business models is not positively and strongly related to the health of the money center banks or the lending firms.

7.3   Lending Firms' Diversification Strategy

The firms comprising the upper arm, which consist almost exclusively of lending firms, are aligned in relative proximity to the upper frontier, identified in the previous section with equality (9). This relative proximity to the upper frontier is reflected by these firms' θ values, which range between 13.7 degrees and 28 degrees. The lending firms' business models constrain the composition of their asset portfolios and limit the extent to which they can diversify. Therefore, as can be expected, lending firms have higher HHI levels—and higher DI values—than money center banks. It is, nevertheless, impossible to infer the lending firms' strategy based on these observations alone. The fact that the lending firms are not aligned along the upper frontier, but rather significantly below it, could be interpreted in two opposite ways. It could suggest, for example, that the lending firms are striving to be as correlated with the aggregate portfolio as their business models permit, yet are compelled to diversify more than they would like to by regulators. Or it could suggest that the lending firms prefer to be as removed as possible from the aggregate portfolio, yet are constrained by their business models. It is hard to tell which of these possible strategies, if any, is behind the lending firms' observed asset portfolio diversification patterns.

The existence of implicit "too many to fail" guarantees could incentivize lending firms to align themselves with the market with the expectation of being bailed out in a time of crisis. Acharya and Yorulmazer (2007) suggest that the larger the number of failed firms, the more likely the regulator is to bail them out in order to avoid continuation losses. The presence of too many to fail guarantees, therefore, has the adverse effect of inducing firms to invest in positively correlated asset portfolios, and hence increases asset commonality driven systemic risk in the financial system. Too many to fail implicit guarantees could explain the lending firms' observed behavior. By adopting similar portfolio diversification patterns, the lending firms might increase their chances of being bailed out in a time of crisis. In Acharya and Yorulmazer (2005) the existence of perceived distress dependencies incentivizes banks to maximize their chances of joint survival by investing in positively correlated asset portfolios. The resulting increased risk of joint failure is overlooked due to the banks' limited liability. It may well be that distress dependencies between the money center banks and the lending firms, and potentially among the lending firms themselves, drive the lending firms to strive to survive together with the market. This strategy also potentially allows the lending firms to benefit from market upswings and better compete with peers.

8. Cluster Analysis and ACRISK

In this section, we use a cluster analysis technique to construct ACRISK, a measure of asset commonality driven systemic risk. Cluster analysis is a statistical data analysis technique for grouping objects according to a measure of dissimilarity and a linkage criterion. In the asset commonality context, we use clustering analysis to separate the firms in our sample, in every given quarter, into clusters based on their asset portfolio composition patterns. A firm has more portfolio composition commonalities with other firms in its cluster than with firms that do not belong to that cluster.

We conduct our analysis in the 16-dimensional simplex projected by the 17 asset classes in our firms' balance sheets as explained in section 2. In that space, the portfolio of a firm in any given period is given by its vector of portfolio weights, $W_{i,t}$. We use an agglomerative hierarchical clustering algorithm, which is a bottom up approach for clustering that starts with each firm being a cluster in its own, and proceeds by merging pairs of existing clusters until all the firms are brought together under one cluster. Our measure of dissimilarity is the elliptical Mahalanobis distance, given by

$$M_{i,j,t} = \sqrt{\left(W_{i,t} - W_{j,t}\right)^T S_{i,j,t}^{-1} \left(W_{i,t} - W_{j,t}\right)}$$

where $S_{i,j,t}^{-1}$ is the covariance matrix for the portfolios of firms i and j in time t. The Mahalanobis distance is a generalization of the Euclidean distance. Our choice of the Mahalanobis distance is motivated by this generalization, which allows us to capture nonspherical clusters. At each stage of the hierarchical clustering process, a linkage criterion is used for choosing the pair of clusters to merge. We apply Ward's minimum variance method, which minimizes the total within-cluster variance, as our linkage criterion.

We visualize the outcome of our clustering exercise for every quarter using a dendrogram. The dendrogram is a tree diagram that illustrates the bottom up formation of clusters by a hierarchical clustering algorithm. Along the horizontal axis we have the firms active in the specific quarter. The vertical axis represents the height, which is the distance (in our case, the Mahalanobis distance) between merged pairs of clusters. The bottom of the dendrogram depicts the starting point of the algorithm, in which each firm is a cluster in its own. The top of the dendrogram is the end point of the algorithm, in which all the firms are bunched together in one cluster. In between are the interim clustering stages, each of which merges pairs of clusters formed at the previous stage. Figure 4 depicts the dendrogram obtained for the first quarter of 2009.

Figure 4. Industry Dendrogram for 2009Q1.

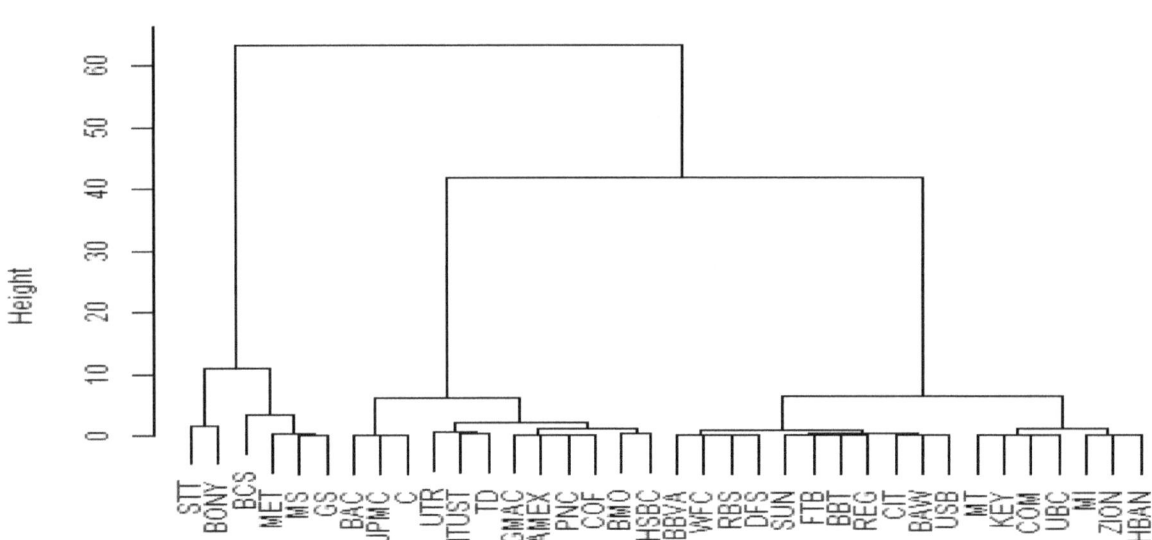

With every stage of the clustering algorithm, the height of the dendrogram increases, as bringing together more firms under one cluster requires a greater distance. Figure 5 depicts the inverse relationship between the number of clusters and the height in our sample in the first quarter of 2009.

Figure 5. Industry Cluster-Height Graph for 2009Q1.

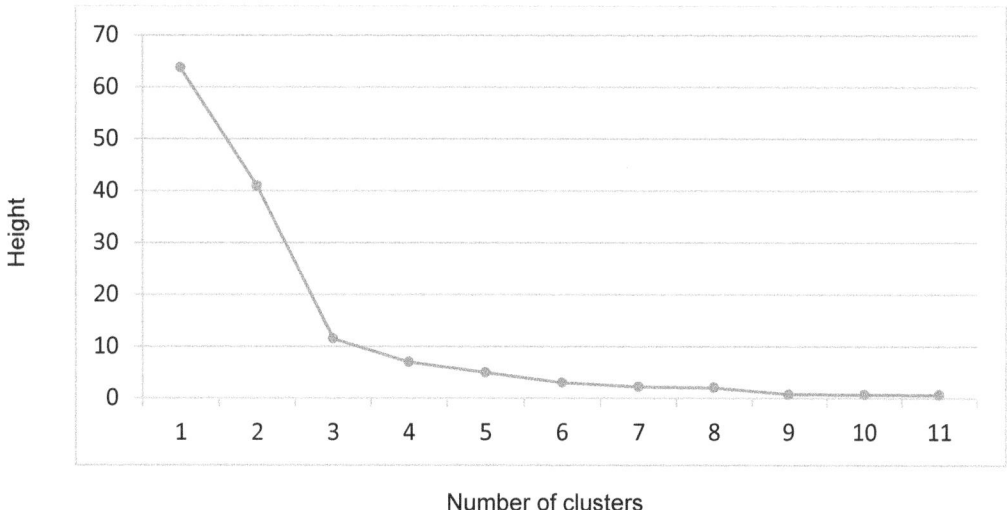

Number of clusters

We construct ACRISK based on the area under the cluster-height graph. Decreasing the number of clusters from *n* to *n-1* involves a height increase. The smaller the height increase, the more overlapping are firms' portfolios. The asset commonality theory implies that greater portfolio overlaps increase systemic risk. Therefore, we expect the size of the area under the cluster-height graph to be inversely related to the systemic risk stemming from asset commonality. This is way we construct ACRISK as the inverse of the area under the cluster height graph, which is bounded between one cluster and five clusters. We choose five clusters as the upper bound on the number of clusters based on our observation that the use of a larger number of clusters has a negligible effect on ACRISK.

Figure 6 shows that ACRISK generally decreased until 2005. Starting in 2005, it steadily increased until it pinnacled in the fourth quarter of 2008, shortly after the collapse of Lehman Brothers.[5] The fourth quarter of 2008 marks a major turning point after which ACRISK sharply decreased, indicating that the system had become less fragile. In the period between the second quarter of 2009 and the fourth quarter of 2011, ACRISK fluctuated around a level significantly higher than any of its pre-2005 levels, and similar to its level in late 2006. This indicates that asset commonality driven systemic risk in that period was not restored to its pre-2005 level. The first two quarters of 2012 then saw a significant decrease in ACRISK, which was followed by a moderate increase up until the end of the sample period in the first quarter of 2013.

---

[5] Lehman Brothers filed for Chapter 11 bankruptcy protection on September 15, 2008.

Figure 6. The Evolution of ACRISK Over the Sample Period.

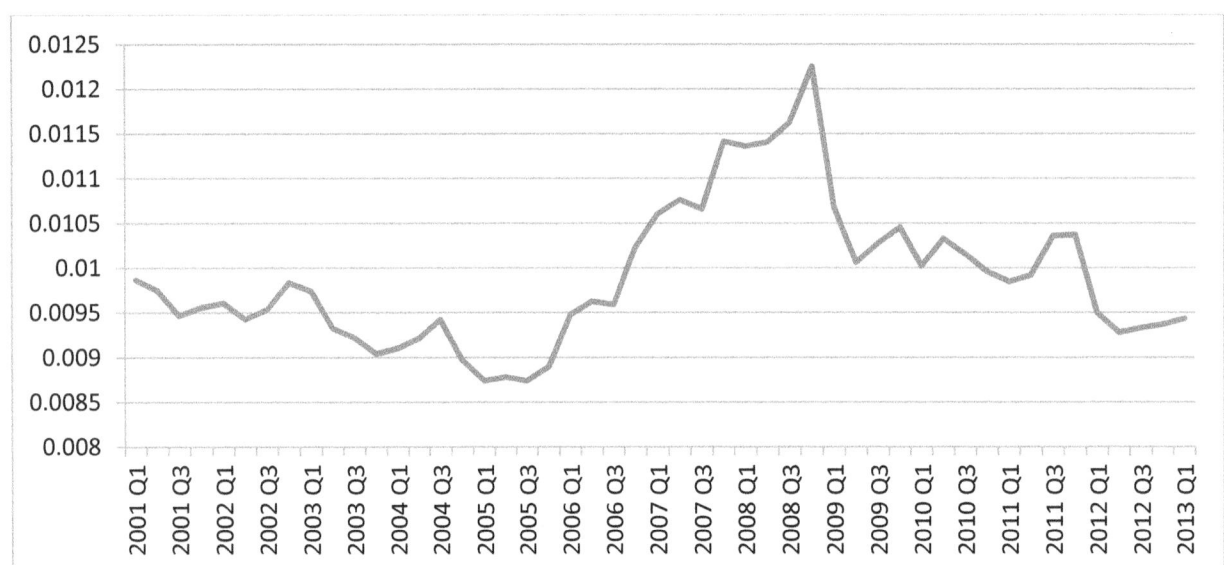

It is important to note that ACRISK cannot be used to capture the contributions of individual firms to asset commonality driven systemic risk. The difference in the ACRISK measure calculated with and without a given firm in the sample would not measure that firm's contribution to systemic risk. That is because removing a firm from the sample would change the aggregate portfolio and the market configuration of the firms in the (DI, HHI) plane. The resulting system would be different from the original one.

9.   Evaluating the Performance of ACRISK

9.1   ACRISK and the Real Economy

Systemic risk typically spills over to the real economy (Acharya et al. [2010a]). ACRISK is designed to capture the buildup of asset commonality driven systemic risk in the financial system, which would make the latter more prone to systemic crises that could impair the real economy. Figure 7 depicts the evolution of ACRISK against the change in U.S. GDP; the change in GDP is inversely related to ACRISK.

Figure 7. The Evolution of ACRISK (Blue, Primary Axis) and the Change in GDP (Green, Secondary Axis) in Billions of Chained 2009 Dollars Over the Sample Period.

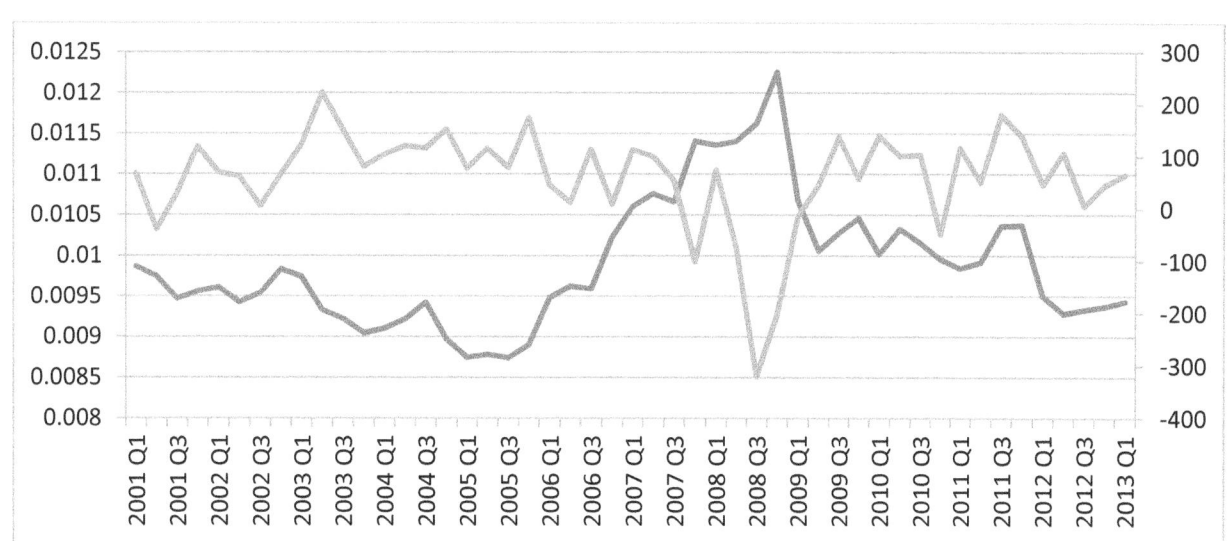

Source for GDP data: the Federal Reserve Bank of St. Louis's FRED database.

9.2 ACRISK Vs. SRISK

Mirroring the multiplicity of interpretations of systemic risk and its many facets, the literature abounds with systemic risk measures. Among the prominent measures in the recent literature is the market based, high frequency MES measure by Acharya et al. (2010b). The MES estimates the propensity of a firm to be undercapitalized when the financial system as a whole is undercapitalized. MES is therefore used to identify the firms that are most vulnerable to a systemic crisis. Engle and Brownlees (2011) supplement the MES with leverage information. The resulting measure, the SRISK index, captures a firm's expected capital shortage given its MES and leverage in times of distress. We obtained historical SRISK daily values for the majority of the firms in our sample from the New York University Stern Volatility Institute[6]. The aggregate SRISK was then obtained by summing the SRISK values of individual firms in the last day of each quarter. The resulting measure is an early warning indicator of system-wide systemic risk. Figure 8 depicts the aggregate SRISK and ACRISK over the sample period. As can easily be seen, ACRISK appears to lead the aggregate SRISK by at least one quarter.

---

[6] We were provided with SRISK data for the 21 largest firms in our sample.

Figure 8. The Evolution of ACRISK (Blue, Primary Axis) and the Aggregate SRISK (Red, Secondary Axis) Over the Sample Period.

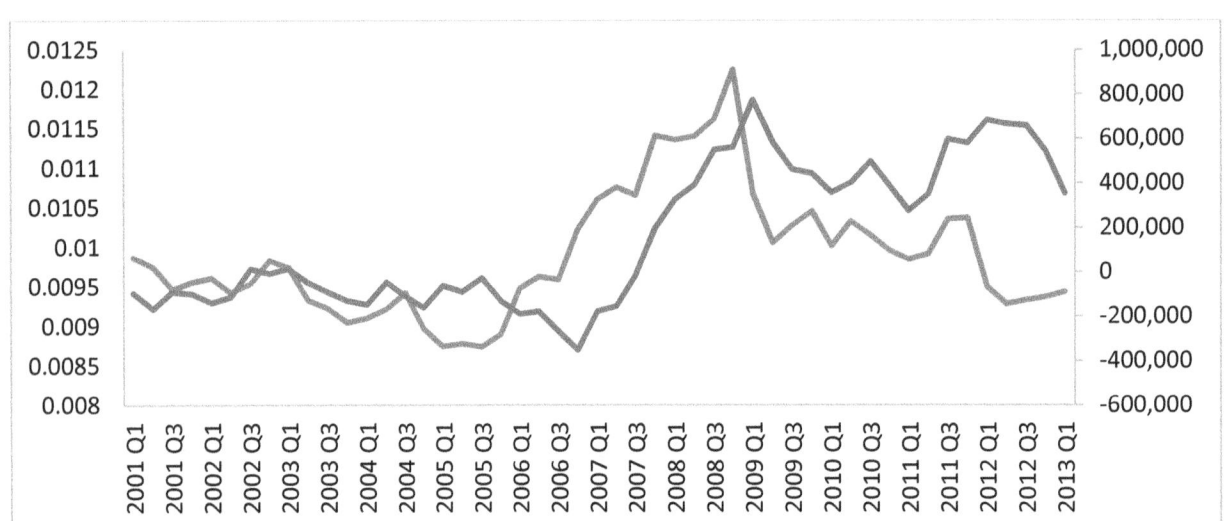

Source for SRISK data: the New York University Stern Volatility Institute.

To get a first gauge of the relationship between the aggregate SRISK and ACRISK, we calculate the correlation between the two measures over the sample period and find it to be 0.42. In addition, we calculate the correlation between the aggregate SRISK and various lagged ACRISK series, ranging from a one-quarter to a six-quarter lag. The results are summarized in table 1. Interestingly, the positive correlation between the aggregate SRISK and lagged ACRISK increases with the number of lags until the four-quarter lag, at which it attains the value of 0.76. The correlation declines as the number of lags increases from that point on.

Table 1. The Correlation Between SRISK and the Lagged ACRISK

Number of quarters by which ACRISK is lagged	Correlation coefficient
1	0.56
2	0.64
3	0.71
4	0.76
5	0.75
6	0.72

We proceed with a Granger causality analysis to test whether ACRISK leads the aggregate SRISK. The Augmented Dickey Fuller test indicates that ACRISK is not stationary at both the level and first difference, whereas the aggregate SRISK is not stationary at the level only. We therefore apply the Granger causality test to the second difference of both measures. The corrected Akaike information criterion suggests that the optimal order of lags in the Granger causality test is one. We find that ACRISK leads the aggregate SRISK: the p-value is 0.023 and the corresponding F statistic is 5.54. Thus, the buildup of asset commonality driven systemic risk captured by ACRISK predicts the expected capital shortage of firms in the system one quarter ahead. This result provides an empirical validation of the asset commonality notion according to which an increase in asset portfolio overlaps across firms would render the financial system more fragile, and hence more prone to systemic crises.

10.   Conclusion

In this paper, we use large BHCs' balance sheet data to analyze asset portfolio composition patterns and construct a measure of asset commonality driven systemic risk in the financial system. We show that when analyzed horizontally, publicly available balance sheet data is informative about the latent buildup of systemic risk. Unlike high frequency, market based measures, low frequency measures do not allow real time monitoring of systemic risk (Rodriguez-Moreno and Pena [2013]). Nevertheless, our balance sheet based measure is invaluable for detecting the buildup of the type of systemic risk that is driven by asset commonalities among firms long before it materializes. Our measure could therefore provide regulators with an important monitoring tool. It is important to emphasize that asset commonality driven systemic risk, which our measure captures, is not the only possible source of systemic risk in the financial system. To obtain a comprehensive picture of systemic risk, regulators should avail themselves of an array of measures, each capturing a different facet of systemic risk.

Due to data availability constraints, we confine ourselves to the universe of BHCs. Ideally we would have liked to include FHCs. More granular balance sheet data in combination with off-balance sheet data would have been more useful. We would have also liked our dataset to cover a longer period of time spanning several business cycles. Nevertheless, the methodology we introduce in this paper can be applied to a more comprehensive dataset should such a database become available. Despite the above data limitations, our ACRISK measure captures well the buildup of systemic risk that culminated in the 2007–2009 global crisis, and leads Engle and Brownlees' high frequency, market based SRISK measure.

Future extensions of our research could take different directions. One direction could focus on understanding the firms' strategies behind our observations: namely, how business model considerations interplay with joint failure risk, idiosyncratic risk, and other factors. Another direction that we find particularly appealing is the inclusion of liabilities side data in the analysis. Given its generality, our methodology lends itself to such extensions. Allen et al. (2012) use a theoretical framework to suggest that the systemic risk imposed by asset commonalities is exacerbated by reliance on short debt maturities. This idea could be empirically tested in future research by supplementing our analysis with balance sheet liability side data. We believe that capturing both sides of the balance sheet could shed light on the systemic liquidity implications of asset commonalities among firms in the financial system.

References

Acharya, V.V., L.H. Pedersen, T. Philippon, and M.P. Richardson, 2010a. "A Tax on Systemic Risk." Working paper, Stern School of Business, Ney York University.

Acharya, V.V., L. H. Pedersen, T. Philippon, and M. P. Richardson, 2010b. "Measuring Systemic Risk." Technical report, department of finance, New York University.

Acharya, V.V., and T. Yorulmazer, 2005. "Limited Liability and Bank Herding." London Business School IFA Working Paper No. 445.

Acharya, V.V., and T. Yorulmazer, 2007. "Too Many to Fail—An Analysis of Time Inconsistency in Bank Closure Policies." *Journal of Financial Intermediation* 16: 1–31.

Allen, F., A. Babus, and E. Carletti, 2012. "Asset Commonality, Debt Maturity and Systemic Risk." *Journal of Financial Economics* 104(3): 519–534.

Allen, F., and D. Gale, 2004. "Financial Fragility, Liquidity, and Asset Prices." *Journal of the European Economic Association* 2(6): 1015–1048.

Beale, N., D.G. Rand, H. Battey, K. Croxson, R.M. May, and M.A. Nowak, 2011. "Individual Versus Systemic Risk and the Regulator's Dilemma." *Proceedings of the National Academy of Sciences* 108(31): 12647–12652.

Billio, M., M. Getmansky, A.W. Lo, and L. Pelizzon, 2010. "Econometric Measures of Systemic Risk in the Finance and Insurance Sectors." Working paper no. w16223, National Bureau of Economic Research.

Bisias, D., M. Flood, A.W. Lo, and S. Valavanis, 2012. "A Survey of Systemic Risk Analytics." *Annual Review of Financial Economics* 4(1): 255–296.

Borio, C., and M. Drehmann, 2009. "Assessing the Risk of Banking Crises—Revisited." *BIS Quarterly Review*, March, 29–46.

Borio, C., and P. Lowe, 2002. "Assessing the Risk of Banking Crises." *BIS Quarterly Review*, December, 43–54.

Ciciretti, R., and R. Corvino, 2012. "How Homogeneous Diversification in Balanced Investment Funds Affects Portfolio and Systemic Risk." *Sovereign Risks*, 65.

De Bandt, O., and P. Hartmann, 2000. "Systemic Risk: A Survey." European Central Bank Working Paper No. 35.

De Jonghe, O., 2010. "Back to the Basics in Banking? A Micro Analysis of Banking System Stability." *Journal of Financial Intermediation* 19(3): 387–417.

De Vries, C.G., 2005. "The Simple Economics of Bank Fragility." *Journal of Banking and Finance* 29, 803-825.

Donoho, D. L., 2000. "High Dimensional Data Analysis: The Curses and Blessings of Dimensionality." Lecture on August 8, 2000, to the American Mathematical Society, "Math Challenges of the 21st Century." Available from www-stat.stanford.edu/~donoho/.

Engle, R., and Brownlees, C. T., 2011. "Volatility, Correlation and Tails for Systemic Risk Measurement." Stern School of Business. Mimeo, New York University.

Fodor, K., 2002. "A Survey of Dimension Reduction Techniques." U.S. Department of Energy.

Huang, X., H. Zhou, and H. Zhu, 2009. "A Framework for Assessing the Systemic Risk of Major Financial Institutions." *Journal of Banking & Finance* 33(11): 2036–2049.

Ibragimov, R., J. Dwight, and J. Walden, 2011. "Diversification Disasters." *Journal of Financial Economics* 99, 333–348.

Lagunoff, R., and S. Schreft, 2001. "A Model of Financial Fragility." *Journal of Economic Theory* 99: 220–264.

Rodriguez-Moreno, M., and J. I. Pena, 2013. "Systemic Risk Measures: The Simpler the Better?" *Journal of Banking & Finance* 37(6): 1817–1831.

San Jose, A., R. Krueger, and P. Khay, 2008. "The IMF's Work on Financial Soundness Indicators." IFC Bulletin No. 28: 33–39.

Schwaab, B., S. J. Koopman, and A. Lucas, 2011. "Systemic Risk Diagnostics, Coincident Indicators and Early Warning Signals." ECB Working Paper No. 1327.

Wagner, W., 2008. "The Homogenization of the Financial System and Financial Crises." *The Journal of Financial Intermediation* 17: 330–56.

Wagner, W., 2009. "Efficient Asset Allocations in the Banking Sector and Financial Regulation." *International Journal of Central Banking* 5, 75–97.

Wagner, W., 2010. "Diversification at Financial Institutions and Systemic Crises." *Journal of Financial Intermediation* 19(3): 373–386.

Appendix

Table A. The 17 Asset Classes for Large U.S. BHCs Used in Our Analysis.

Asset class #	Asset class
1	Non-interest bearing balances
2	Interest bearing balances in the United States
3	Interest bearing balances in foreign offices
4	Securities held to maturity
5	Securities available for sale
6	Fed funds sold in domestic offices
7	Fed funds securities purchased under agreements to resell
8	Loans and leases held for sale
9	Loans and leases net unearned income
10	Trading assets
11	Premises and fixed assets
12	Other real estate owned
13	Investments in unconsolidated subsidiaries
14	Direct and indirect investments in real estate
15	Goodwill
16	Other intangibles
17	Other assets

Source: PRISM

www.ingramcontent.com/pod-product-compliance
Lightning Source LLC
Chambersburg PA
CBHW080625180526
45168CB00007B/3062